African Women's Wisdom

Original Parables
Based On African Proverbs
To Empower The Feminine

Queen Mother Yaa Asantewaa 1840 – 1921

Child-Time Publishers

Established 1988

www.childtimepublishers.com

Library of Congress Number: 2017907779

First Edition: May 2017

ISBN: 978-0-929934-03-7

Cover Art: Sabina K. Mintz

W.o.W Logo: Sabina K. Mintz & Eric Sander Kingston

Printed In USA

W.o.W.

Wish On Wisdom tm

There was once a person, who was granted from Heaven, a wish. They could either wish for wealth, or wish for wisdom. The person replied: "I wish for wisdom. For through wisdom, I will attain great wealth."

A Note On The Cover:

*"Queen Mother
Yaa Asantewaa
The woman who
fights before
cannons
You have
accomplished
great things
You have done
well."*

Yaa Asantewaa was a human rights activist, a Queen and a courageous, powerful leader. She promoted women's emancipation and stood for gender equality. Yaa Asantewaa led the Ashanti rebellion to defend the area known as the Golden stool. She insisted that if the men would not fight, she would mobilize the African women to stand and fight for their land. She is considered at the top of Africa's greatest female leaders.

It is my hope, that someone out there will research this woman, Queen Yaa Asantewaa, and create a modern film based upon this woman's courage, honor and sacrifice for her people.

A Woman of Valor

Dedicated to the women who showed me what true strength is

A woman of valor makes the world change
Her strength is the content that guides through the day
Defined by her actions that brings light to all dreams
Valor is something that's defined by her deeds

Her valor is golden, sparkled and gray
She stands up to the challenge no matter life's way
She can't be held back or defined by her age
Yes, a woman of valor makes the world change

For valor's not held by the young or the old
But by the deeds of her heart that give and unfold
Her merit and honor hold no disguise
Like the creation of being in the blessed Holy One's
Eyes

For valor is the color of the song of her soul
As she changes, creates and turns light into gold
Divine is Her Presence, be it joyous or sad
— A Woman of Valor —
May offer little, but it will be all that she has
For only her heart will know the depths of her soul
That nurtures and blossom and forever unfolds
And holds in its essence new life and new gain
Yes,
A woman of valor makes the world change
A woman of valor makes the world change
A woman of valor makes the world change

Eric Sander Kingston

<u>Wish On Wisdom Philosophy</u>

I believe in celebrating and cultivating the great wisdom's contained within each and every culture. The "Wish On Wisdom" parable series, seek to share the wisdom and spiritual lessons, that all races, religions and regions have to offer humanity.

The lessons contained within the parables, I believe, are universal, and transcend beyond the "lens" of the particular culture, we chose to focus upon. With that stated, the parables are not limited to any race, religion or region. These parables, are meant to be interactive, and have a flexibility. Our deepest purpose, is to share the wisdom, of every race, religion and region to create bridges of unity, and mutual respect and understanding, between all peoples of our planet earth.

"Our most basic common link, is that we all inhabit this planet. We all breathe the same air. We all cherish our children's future, and we are all mortal."

John F. Kennedy

With Humanity In Thought,

Eric Sander Kingston

The parables within this book, as mentioned, are meant to teach insights and no particular flaw is being pointed at the masculine, or the male of ANY culture. The power is contained within individuals, within the "content of their character" as Dr. Martin Luther King, Jr. Stated, and not in skin colors, religion, male or female.

To All Women Everywhere:

Remember who you were.

See who you are.

Become again, what you born to be.

Table Of Contents

The Bridge

Written For Izzy Malin & Published In The Booklet
Honoring Coretta Scott King (Dr. Martin Luther King,
Jr.s Widow)   Special Thank You To Rev. Kenneth
Flowers

Togetherness connects and crosses all lines

It brings us together in humanities ties

When joined in our struggles to help and to give

Then hand-in-hand we will cross every bridge

For friends of today must bridge towards tomorrow

No matter the cost, or the loss, or the struggle

For those who stand with us and those yet to be saved

We must give of the soul for the bridge to be made

If each can contribute to humanities path

Then we can bind all our faiths to eventually pass

For ideas can't be broken no matter our loss

When we unite in the heart any bridge can be crossed

For what brings us together is not what divides

That's only illusions that keep heart from mind

But someday we'll join beyond our tears and our loss

And without fear the bridge will be crossed!

There was once a mother, who lived by the side of a vast rock mountain. Her daughter, who was also her best friend, lived a great distance away. Each day the mother wished, deep within her heart, to see and embrace her child again. Yet, this was not an easy wish for the mother to fulfill, for her daughter was living on the other side of the vast rock mountain, from where the mother lived. One day, the mother chose to stop only wishing about seeing her daughter, and made a plan to go on the journey to be with her. The people who lived around the mother, told her that she would have to cross through the thick of the forest, and over the treacherous, vast mountain of rock, to get there. Constantly, she was being told that it was impossible, but this mother did not care. The day came, and she went into action, packed what she could, and began her arduous journey. When she arrived at edge of the forest, she was again warned that it was impossible, and too dangerous to take this journey, but it did not matter, through the forest she went. Then, she came upon the vast mountain of rock. At the base of the mountain, she was once again warned by a man, that it was impossible to get over this rock mountain alone, but those words did not matter. She just continued in steadfast action, for nothing would stop this mother from embracing her beloved and best friend again. She forged, on and on and over the top of the rock mountain she went. Finally, after a few days more, she descended down the other side of the mountain, and stood at its base. In the near distance, she could see her beloved daughter. The daughter, seeing her mother, ran and embraced her. An astonished man was standing at the base of the mountain. He then approached the mother, and asked how she was able to accomplish such an arduous journey alone, where most others fail to succeed. Standing there, holding her daughter within her arms, she did not need to say a word. For she was living testimony, through power of motherhood, to the Ashanti Proverb…

"You must act as if it is impossible to fail."

Insight: Our belief is more powerful than circumstance or condition when we GO into action.

Question: Where could you use your power of belief, to achieve an action to accomplish an intended goal?

Agreement: I, _____, agree and commit to, for myself, to believing my own inner-power can overcome many conditions and circumstance.

Do What You Can

There was once a young woman, who some judged as nothing very special. Yet, this woman possessed a true internal power. A power, that shined within the belief of who she was, and what she could do with her own hands. One day, she chose to go after her dream, a dream that many people thought were way, way beyond her reach. Yet, those people did not understand, that this was a woman of deep internal determination, a woman who deeply understood the powers she was able to manifest to create the destiny, she held within her own hands. Anytime people, or events, tried to make her look at areas in her life, that contained things she could not ever do, or ever needed to do; she would remind herself that: You judge the possibilities of an eagle, by how well it uses its wings to fly, not on how well it can swim. From that wisdom, she stayed focused upon her belief in her dreams and what she herself COULD DO with her own hands. Years later, this woman did achieve her dream, and much, much more, and was living testimony to the Ashanti proverb…

"Do not let what you cannot do,
tear from your hands, what you can do."

Insight: By staying focused on what can be accomplish from your own hands, you can achieve your dreams.

Question: Where could you be allowing what you do not have (or need), to interfere with what you do have and can do?

Agreement: I, _____, agree and commit to, for myself, to holding on and staying focused to those qualities I can utilize within my life.

Inedible Diamonds

One day, a man who sought precious gems in the caves of Africa, got very lucky. The man, found several precious large diamonds. He excitedly ran home and showed his wife of his good fortune. She was very elated, and began to speak of all the things they could now do and buy. She said, "Let us tomorrow feast!!!" The man agreed, but as the night went on, he could not sleep. He just stared, and stared, at the precious glittering diamonds he had found. Night after night, he did this. Many days went by, but he would not part with the gems, and hoarded them. His wife became frustrated, because the man would not sell the diamonds, even though they were living in near poverty condition. Finally, the man chose to leave his wife. He charted a small boat with some funds, and went to find somewhere else to live. He set sail, but during the journey a storm arose, and capsized the boat, destroying it. The man would have drowned, if he had not managed to grab onto a piece of the boats floating wood. He drifted, until he ended up on a small deserted island, which contained nothing but sand and stones. After suffering many days of hunger, he thought of his loving wife, and her words "let us feast". With his last bit of will, he pulled out of his pocket, the small bag of (inedible) diamonds, finally understanding the Ghana Proverb…

"You should not hoard your wealth and die of hunger."

Insight: Wealth is not in the object, but how we utilize what have.

Question: Where could you use your knowledge, wealth and/or love in a less isolated way of being?

Agreement: I, _____, agree and commit to, for myself, to share and use my assists in a more open powerful way.

Beautiful Wisdom

There was once family, who had a very large, lucrative farm. They had one daughter, who was very, very beautiful. When she got old enough, her mother began teaching her about hard work and farming. Other families would tell her, that, "with your daughter's beauty, she will not have to ever work!" The mother knew better, and continued to teach her daughter about work. A year later, the family's farm burnt to almost nothing. The parents, who were now too old to work, did not know what to do. They were afraid they would all lose everything and starve, but the very beautiful daughter took over. She, through her good work and effort, and using the wisdom her mother had imparted within her, rebuilt the family farm, proving the wisdom of the Congo proverb...

"You are beautiful, but learn to work,
for you cannot eat your beauty."

Insight: External beauty, without inner substance, can only take you so far.

Question: Where could you be placing too much emphasis upon the externals?

Agreement: I, _____, agree and commit to, for myself, to developing a strong work ethic.

From Bitter Water To Honey Wine

One day, a woman walked deep into the wilderness, and got lost. For many days, she wandered. The more time that passed by, the lonelier she became. Finally, she found a small river and sat down alone, and wept. She became thirsty, so she reached over and cupped some of the rivers water with her hand. She then drank it. Yet, the water seemed to be very bitter. In her loneliness, she thought how much sweetness the water lacked. Suddenly, she heard footsteps approaching. She became afraid, but then she saw not a stranger, but her true and loving friend, who had been seeking after her. The friend walked over, and they embraced. The two friends, then drank from the river, which had seemed to transform, from bitter waters into honey wine, confirming the African proverb...

"Between true friends, even water drunk together is sweet enough."

Insight: Loving and caring friends transform lives in times of loss and loneliness.

Question: Where in my life could I open my heart to a friend who feels lost and lonely?

Agreement: I,_____, agree and commit to, for myself, to seeing the sweetness of true friends as vessels of transformation.

The Stones Of Love

There was once a very handsome prince, who was seeking a woman to become his princess. A woman from a distant province knew she was the one. Those around this woman, told her that she was average, and not very good to look at. They told her that many beautiful women were after the prince. Finally, they said "It is impossible!!! It would be like trying to move a giant stone mountain!" Yet, this woman was unmoved by their comments. So, she moved as close as she could to the prince. Each day, the prince would walk through the town, where this woman was now living. Each day, she would try to give the prince, a flowered yellow rose, as he passed by. One day, the prince accepted the first of her roses. From then on, she would give the prince a rose, each day, as he walked through the town. It came to pass, that the prince started to speak with this woman. This went on for some time: Rose by rose, like removing stones, one at a time from a mountain, the woman's flowers, and intelligent soft words, started to create an opening within the prince's heart that deeply moved him. He had, by now, grown quite fond of her. Then, on one particular walk through the town, the woman was not there. The prince felt something amiss, so he sought after her and her flowers. He searched, until finally, he found her, by a mountain of yellow roses. As he embraced her, the prince also found in this woman, his princess, for this woman proved true the virtue of the African proverb…

*"If you want to move mountains tomorrow,
you must start by moving stones today."*

Insight: With patience and process many things, others believe impossible, can be achieved.

Question: Are there any areas in your life, where you are trying to move mountain's all at once, instead of using step-by-step wisdom?

Agreement: I, _____, agree and commit to, for myself, to seeing the "unmovable mountains" in my life, as just stones that can be moved one by one.

100% Of Nothing
A Mother's Wisdom

There was once, a very old wise mother, who had two strong, intelligent, but headstrong sons. Their father had passed away long ago, but had willed to them a very, very large estate, that would someday go to them. One day, the mother called her sons into her room to speak with her. She was now very old, and about to pass onto the other side. As the mother spoke, each son listened, and each held one of the hands of his mother. Then, the mother told her sons, that it was her wish, that they should share the vast estate, that would now be left to them. She also wished for them to do good deeds for the community. Then, the mother passed away. The sons immediately let go of the mother's hands. Each looked at the other with contempt. Stepping outside onto the vast estate, they began to argue over who should get what part of this vast valuable land. Ignoring the wisdom of their mother, they began to fight. They fought so viciously, that one grabbed a shovel, and the other a large stick. Finally, they destroyed each other. A few months later, a stranger took control of their vast land, proving true the Ibo proverb…

"When brothers fight to the death,
a stranger inherits their father's estate."

Insight: When our love gets blinded by greed, we inherit 100% of nothing, instead of sharing a percentage of the riches.

Question: Are there any areas of your life where greed is over-shadowing your sense of humanity?

Agreement: I, _____, agree and commit to, for myself, to seeing and embracing, the love between myself and others, no matter the circumstance.

Unsightly Beauty

One day, a Queen-less King was very sad. So, he chose to slip away from his castle, and wander into the surrounding forest. Finally, he came upon a vast dark cave. Wandering into it, the King got lost. No matter what the King did, he could not find his way out of the cave. He just continued searching in the darkness, until suddenly, he heard the voice of a woman singing. The King thought to himself, this is the most beautiful voice I have ever heard. So, he followed the voice until he found the woman. Surprised to see someone else in the cave of darkness, the woman asked the King what he was doing here. The King said that he was lost and could not find his way out. The King then inquired if the woman was lost within this cave too. She said that she chose to live in this cave of darkness and to stay here. The King then told the woman, that he was actually the King of the land, and if she assisted him in finding his way out of this cave of darkness, he would reward her greatly. She agreed. For days they wandered, and as they wandered, they spoke. The King was very taken by this woman's wisdom, insights and understanding. He had been acquainted with many beautiful women in his day, but never felt the intimacy he was now experiencing. Finally, the King asked why he chose to live in this cave. The woman replied that she was very unsightly to look upon. Just as she said that, the opening of the cave appeared, and light filled it with the rays of the rising sun. The King then turned to look upon the woman's transformed face, and he knew she would never be alone again, for this woman's beauty outshone any woman the King had ever known before, proving the Ganda Proverb...

> *"The one who loves an unsightly person,*
> *is the one who makes them beautiful."*

Insight: When the beauty that shines within, is loved by another, the external appearance transforms.

Question: Where in your life could you see beyond only the superficial externals of others and into the true beauty contained within?

Agreement: I, _____, agree and commit to, for myself, to focusing more upon the inner-beauty within others and myself.

A Wise Woman And An Impatient Man

There was once a husband and wife, who were selling their home to move near the sea, to begin anew. To also help finance their journey, they had sold many things they had collected throughout the years. They had placed all the money from those sales, into a large bag. The night before the final sale of their home, it got to be very cold in their house. The fire, in their fireplace, which usually glowed bright, was nothing more than some glowing red coals. The wife said to her husband, get another blanket, and let us just lay in bed like when we were young. The husband said he had a bag of kindling, and would quickly build up the fire again. The wife said, that it would take time, and that it was almost morning anyway, so let us just lay together and dream. Yet, the husband still wanted a fire. A disagreement arose. Finally, the husband jumped out of their bed and ran over to the fire place tossing the whole bag of kindling, which lay next to the fireplace, into it. The bag burst into flames. Unfortunately, it was not the kindling, but the bag of money, which contained all their savings. The money flew out ablaze from the fireplace, and quickly turned the whole house into flame. The couple ran out, and within an hour, the money and home, were burnt to the ground, as the man learned the wisdom of the African proverb…

"He who burns down his house knows why ashes cost a fortune."

Insight: Patience and love, keep the flames of emotion safely contained in the heart.

Question: Where could you need to become more understanding and patience?

Agreement: I, _____, agree and commit to, for myself, to seeing the internal fire of patience and love, contain the true light.

The Poor Rich Woman

There was once a very wealthy woman, who owned a house of gold. She was very proud of its appearance and value. One day, she hired a less fortunate woman, to clean her vast home. Yet, even after years, the owner of the home remained very stringent, and spoke very little, except to give orders or see business associates. The woman, whom the wealthy woman hired, kept quiet each day as she did her required chores. Yet, each night in her humble home, she met with her family and friends, spending the evenings laughing and dancing. One day, this simple woman did not show to work. The wealthy woman who employed her, became upset. So, she chose to go to this woman's home, whom she employed, to find the reason for her absence. When she was just about there, she suddenly realized it was the African Holiday of Kwanza. She felt strangely alone, as she walked through the neighborhoods of singing joyful homes. Finally, she found the woman's home of whom she employed. Yet, when she peered in through the window, she saw not the quiet little cleaning woman, but a woman of valor, whose family and friends adored her. She realized, in that moment, that she herself had no real friends, and returning alone, to her empty house of gold, she no longer saw its value, and she wept, finally understanding the Tanzanian proverb…

"To be without a friend is to be poor indeed."

Insight: There are many forms of poverty beyond not having money.

Question: How could you use what you do have to create deeper friendships?

Agreement: I, _____, agree and commit to, for myself, to seeing true friendship, and being open hearted as a form of great wealth.

The Lovely Demon

A hardworking man had a very honorable and educated wife. Yet, he worked so hard that he had little time for study. His pious wife came from a very educated village. Each night, she would take time from her own busy day, to share with her husband, the heartfelt wisdom and teachings, of her ancestor's ways. The husband would say he did not have much interest in learning through her teaching. He sought only to learn through living the experience. The wife would try and tell her husband, that all life is learning, and we can learn through both forms: experience and the wisdom of another's teaching. She also told him, that the unwise often have to learn lessons, especially lessons of the heart, the hard way. A few months, later this man saw a very beautiful woman. Each day he saw her on his way to work. After a while, he began talking with her. He felt, this woman, possessed the beauty of dove. This woman, told him that she lived in a crystal cave by herself, and that the man should come visit her one evening. That very night, he snuck away from his wife and home. He soon found the woman's cave. As he entered her domain, he saw her even more beautiful than ever. He ran and embraced her. Yet, as they embraced, the crystal cave turned to stone and became darkened. It was then, the man saw this woman's true nature, not that of a beautiful dove, but of a possessed, wild hungry leopard. He thought of his wife's heartfelt wisdom, and as she attacked with cat's eyes, he learned the true meaning of the Baluba proverb...

"The skin of the leopard is beautiful, but not its heart."

Insight: Sometimes, it is better to learn a lesson through a shared teaching, than a hard experience.

Question: Where could you be choosing to learn a lesson the hard way?

Agreement: I, _____, agree and commit to, for myself, to value learning through the wisdom of others as well as experience.

A Way To The King

There was once a very lonely King, of a large estate, who was seeking a Queen to be his wife. Within the King's vast kingdom, there were two very eligible women, both of great, great beauty. Hearing of the King's yearning for a Queen, they both sought to find a way to meet the King. One of the women, prepared by garnering beautiful dresses, and adorning herself with jewels, and perfumes. The other women, did not concern herself as much with the external beauty, but rather, focused upon the wisdom of the lands elders, and understanding the ways and traditions of the King. One day, these two women were invited to meet with the King. After a short wait, they were both escorted into the King's chamber. Yet, just as the visit began, a local official ran in, and brought up a serious issue to the King that had just arose in the land. The King quickly called in his advisers and asked what they recommended to do, but they were uncertain. Finally, the woman who had focused upon the wisdom of her elders, and the traditions of the King, gave the King the perfect solution. The King, seeing her great value, and internal worth, chose her as his Queen, proving the Tanzanian proverb…

"A wise person will always find a way."

Insight: Wisdom has a beauty and power all its own.

Question: Are there areas in your life, where you believe external beauty alone is enough?

An Agreement: I, _____, agree and commit to, for myself, to further developing my inner wisdom and understanding the roots from where I came.

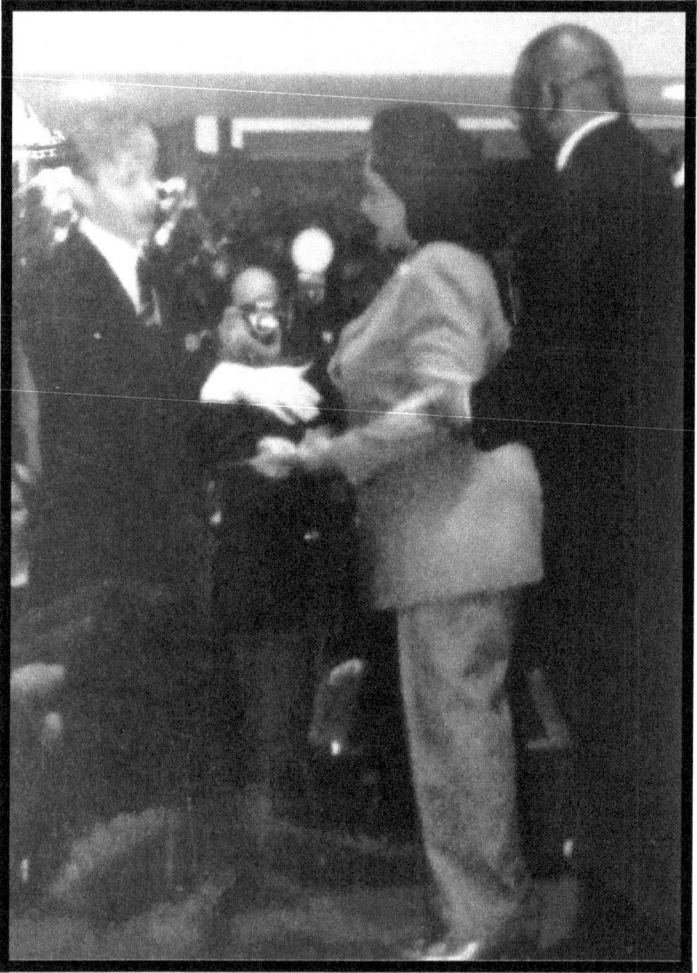

Presenting my work, "Faith, Love & Tolerance" To Coretta Scott King (Dr. Martin Luther King, Jr.s widow). *See Essay*

Faith, Love & Tolerance

Inspired By Dr. Martin Luther King, Jr.

"It has always been a mystery to me,
how men could feel themselves honored
by the humiliation of the fellow beings."
Mahatma Gandhi

In a world filled with duality and intolerance, faith and love are not easy philosophies to completely unify one's life by. Each day, to some extent, requires an individual to re-affiliate their own selves with the unique qualities, and positive energies, of what faith and love will one day manifest upon the face of the earth: a world of enduring peace and global understanding between all races, regions and religions.

For us to reach that day, it will surely take a combined overall effort, but we as individuals can create, and speedup that days arrival, by committing ourselves to a more unified way of tolerance, and internal understanding towards one another's positive ways of being.

Understandably, to reach this goal, will require a daily commitment to ourselves, not only others. Each day we rise up, and every night we lay down, we would do well to cultivate the deep awareness, that faith, love and tolerance are not clichéd ideals, but rather, life's salvational tools, and keystones, whose vibratory energy, penetrate and widen, even the smallest cracks in the walls of tyranny and injustice. We would also do well to understand, that no matter the challenge before us, we must stay committed to these forms of human energies, because history has shown us, that as these cracks in the walls of tyranny and injustice widen, so do the possibilities of manifesting a stronger today and a brighter tomorrow, that will ultimately create, for each of us, a history of a hand-in-hand unified humanity of peace and tolerance.

There are those among us, who will still choose to live with walls of fear and intolerance, who will have mistrust of their fellows, who will exist in limited ways of thought and action, but each day we can remember, "even for a moment," that even in the darkest souls of oppression and anger, somewhere in that human heart, there dwells the need to belong, the yearning to be understood, and the want to be recognized as a complete, and sovereign, human being.

Ultimately, the Promised Land, is not a place of state, but a state of mind. A state built upon the pillars of faith, and unified by the empathetic understanding, that we are all Children of a Higher Source. With that in mind, we can remain steadfast, to the internal wisdom, that the true seeds of a faithful, tolerance and loving humanity, have merely been covered by the thin dusts of injustice, the limited veils of tyranny, and the false mask of hatred, by which the winds of global acceptance, Divine Wisdom and universal tolerance, will one day, forever wash clean.

So everyday, no matter our burden, let us try and remember, that we are never alone in life's struggle. That in our world, exist those who are of true Universal Will, those who struggle to live by the creed of a faith, that is wide enough to openly accept differences, a love, that is big enough to forgive and a charitable and tolerant way, that is open to new possibilities and unified potentials.

Let us always remember, in times of despair, of those who seek to go beyond the boundaries of their region, who live beyond the prejudices of skin tones, and who do not see life as limited by their particular way of being. I speak of those, who, no matter how small or insignificant, their contributions may, on the surface seem, believe that the nucleus of a faith, love and tolerant reality, is created, step-by-step, through courageous daily actions, to go beyond the preconditioned destructive thought-forms of racism, intolerance and fear based terror. I speak of those who choose to live in accordance with the challenges and energies of faith and love and tolerance.

Therefore, let us keep in mind, that much of our life is a choice, and that the middle word of life is "if", and when the convictions of our faith and love and tolerance, are combined with thought and action, they become powerful seeds of change, that become the living, breathing, instruments which can transform even the perceived common person into a saint. For once the seeds of a tolerant faith and love, are implanted and brought forth from the grounds of human direction; they create powerful realities that bring into existence, what we once thought of as only far off hope and idealistic dreams. This is the choice, and challenge, laid before each individual each day.

Yet, for us as a humanity, to reach this united way of being, it will require a combined effort, as well as our own individual commitment, to forge these potentials and dream-possibilities, into this unified, viable living reality.

So let us commit today and everyday, to being one with the "better angels of our nature." Let us all walk together, towards the cleansing waters of humanity as brothers and sisters, and let us bring together a unified wave of tolerance and global understanding: A wave strong enough to wash clean and nurture, the covered, yet always available, seeds of faith, love and tolerance that only require our commitment to their actions, to become living realities. Let us do this, not as individuals contained within the restrictive lines of race, region and religion, but as G-d's Chosen Creations, as individuals all connected to that One common Soul, that One Soul that still says: "Rise, rise up together as one, with a new-found strength to wash forever clean the stained walls of cynicism and intolerance, and as we nurture the grounds of freedom, going beyond the illusion that says we no longer require, as a cornerstone of humanity, a world based on faith, love, character and a universal acceptance to fully exist, and evolve peacefully with one another: Let us all; finally, embrace the self-evident truth, that we sharing this small planet, are all G-d's Children: Created equally, born equally, united by blood, ruled by G-d and driven for humanity.

With Our Freedom & Humanity In Thought,
Eric Sander Kingston

Power Of One

Song For Africa

We were sitting by the rivers of silence
When they took us by surprise
We seen our own brothers cut down
Right before our eyes

But one day I'm gonna be happy
Just wait and see
One day I'm gonna be happy
When I am free
When I am free
When I am free
When this worlds how its supposed to be
When I am free
When I am free
When this worlds how its suppose to be

Holy children are lost on G-d's Land
Brothers and sister's who can't understand
Nothing but persecution lays all around
Sticks fighting guns on warm blood soaked grounds

They've driven a stake through the heart of my land
Erected their fences to separated man
But they cannot take our hears and souls away
For each of us carries each others pain

Brothers and sisters we must unite
To tear down the fences we must unite
Beyond all religions
Beyond black or white
There is a place where all things are light

But one day I'm gonna be happy
Just wait and see
One day I'm gonna be happy
When I am free
When I am free
When I am free
When this worlds how its supposed to be
When I am free
When I am free
When this worlds how its suppose to be

The rains coming to cool down this land
To wash away the tears of the innocent man
Mothers and daughters and fathers and sons
We've got to believe in the power of one
Yes,
We've got to believe in the power of onc
We've got to believe in life's daughters and sons
All around you may see nothing but pain
But from the heavens fall cool cleansing rain

One day I'm gonna be happy
You can't hold us down
One day I'm gonna be happy
One day is now
One day is now
One day is NOW

Words & Music Eric Sander Kingston

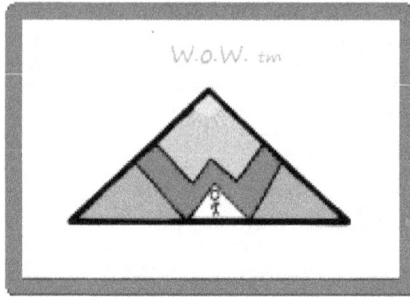

W.O.W. tm

<u>Wish On Wisdom</u>

Wish on Wisdom is a book series, created by Eric Sander Kingston, for the purpose of sharing the wisdom contained in every race around our world, through original writings, music and film. Become A Part Of This

ericsanderkingston.com
wishonwisdom.com

ABOUT ERIC SANDER KINGSTON

Eric Sander Kingston is a Master Level Martial Artist, teacher, writer and composer who currently resides in Los Angeles, California.

Eric's Martial Arts system, books and philosophy empower people to breakthrough their duality, fears, and cultivate a deep, internal power of awareness, allowing them greater access to achieve their purpose and cultivate a life of stability and sustainable success in multiple realms.

www.ericsanderkingston.com

www.ingramcontent.com/pod-product-compliance
Lightning Source LLC
Chambersburg PA
CBHW060626030426
42337CB00018B/3222

* 9 7 8 0 9 2 9 9 3 4 0 3 7 *